The Cryptocurrency Adventure for Kids: An Exciting Journey into the World of Bitcoin and Ethereum!

Author Kwame

Once upon a time, in a land far, far away, there was a special type of money called "cryptocurrency."

It was different from the money that Mommy and Daddy use to buy things, like toys and ice cream.

Cryptocurrency is a digital or virtual currency that uses special computer code to keep it secure.

One of the most popular types of cryptocurrency is called "Bitcoin." It was created in 2009 by a person or group of people using the name Satoshi Nakamoto.

People use Bitcoin just like they would use regular money to buy things online.

But it's also special because it can be bought and sold on special websites called "exchanges."

Chapter 3:
The Magic of Blockchain

The technology that makes Bitcoin possible is called "blockchain."

It's like a big digital book that keeps track of every single Bitcoin transaction that has ever happened.

Each page in this digital book is called a "block," and it's linked to all the other pages, creating a "chain."

Blockchain Technology

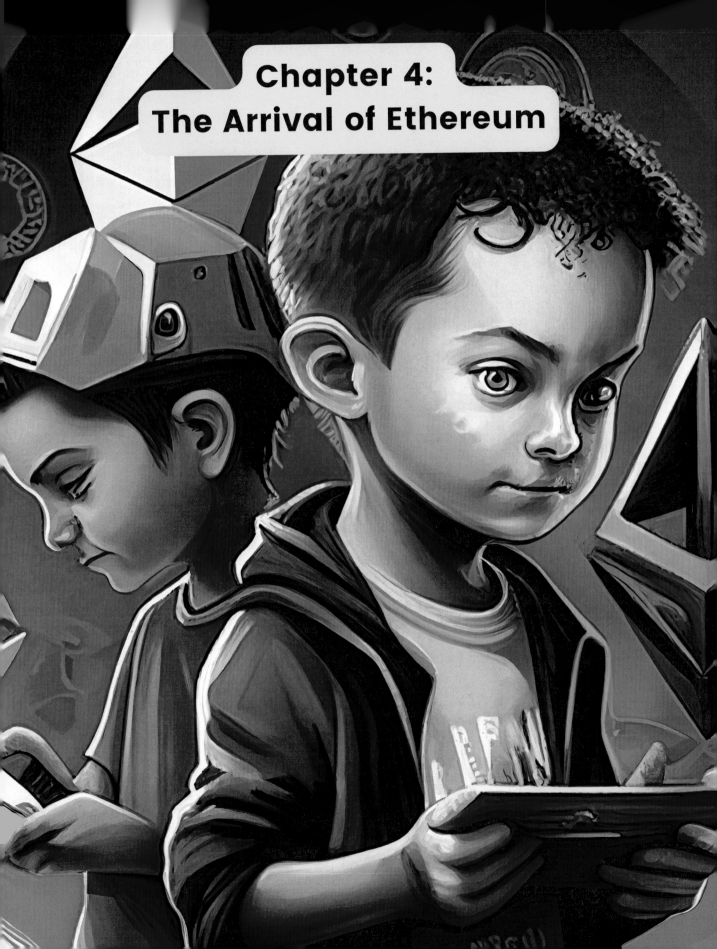

Chapter 4:
The Arrival of Ethereum

Another popular cryptocurrency is called "Ethereum" or "ETH" for short. It was created in 2015 by a person named Vitalik Buterin.

Ethereum is similar to Bitcoin in that it can be used to buy things and traded on exchanges.

It's also special because it allows people to create their own digital assets and programs called "smart contracts" on top of the Ethereum blockchain.

Chapter 5:
Keeping Your Cryptocurrency Safe

Both Bitcoin and Ethereum are stored in a digital wallet, which is like a virtual piggy bank. You can send and receive Bitcoin and Ethereum just like you would send an email.

It's important to keep your digital wallet safe and only use it with people and places that you trust.

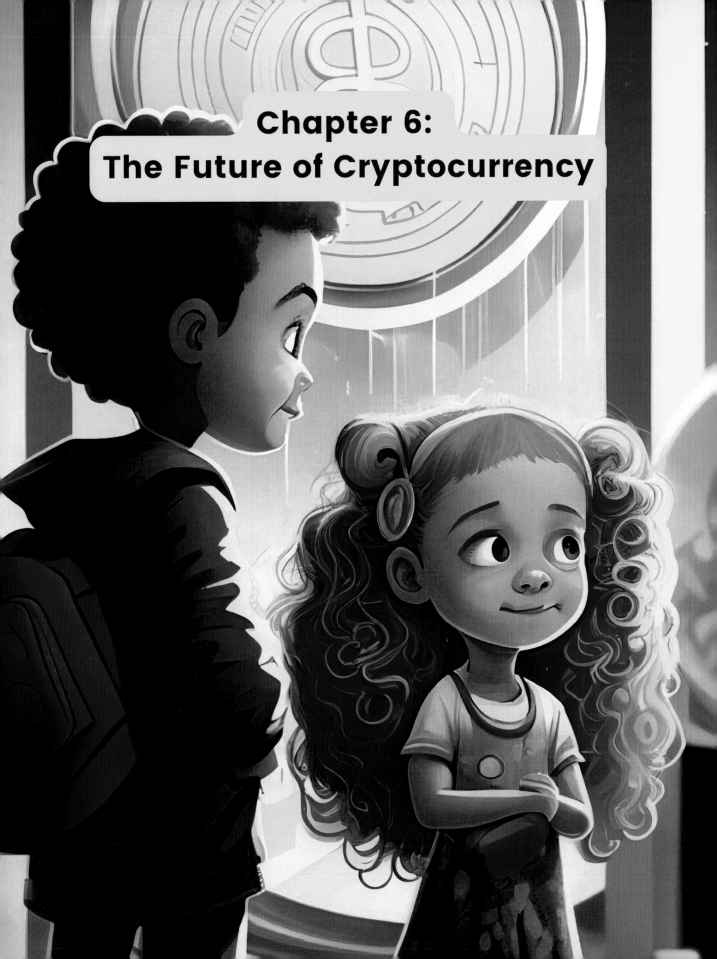

Chapter 6:
The Future of Cryptocurrency

Nowadays, more and more businesses are starting to accept Bitcoin and Ethereum as a form of payment.

Some people even use them to invest and save for the future, just like stocks or real estate.

The future of

cryptocurrency is bright

and full of possibilities!

Cryptocurrency is a

magical and exciting

type of money.

Just like any type of money, it's important to be careful and only use it with people and places that you trust.

Always ask Mommy or

Daddy before using

Bitcoin, Ethereum or any

other cryptocurrency.

BOOK

THE END.